IMAGES OF ENGLAND

BELPER
AND
MILFORD

IMAGES OF ENGLAND

BELPER
AND
MILFORD

ADRIAN FARMER

TEMPUS

In memory of George Barrass, Cyril Maskery and Arthur Bellaby, who contributed so much to the preservation and telling of Belper's past. Also Maud Hoult, who sparked my own interest in the past.

Frontispiece: Sitting outside one of the cottages which once stood between Belper's North Mill and the weir are John Davis and his wife. Behind them in their grotto of seashells is a sign proclaiming: John Davis. Born 6 August 1818. My temple borne of toil and thought, seeks but to please and amuse for nought.

First published 2004

Tempus Publishing Limited
The Mill, Brimscombe Port,
Stroud, Gloucestershire, GL5 2QG
www.tempus-publishing.com

© Adrian Farmer, 2004

The right of Adrian Farmer to be identified as the Author
of this work has been asserted in accordance with the
Copyrights, Designs and Patents Act 1988.

British Library Cataloguing in Publication Data.
A catalogue record for this book is available from the British Library.

ISBN 0 7524 3376 8

Typesetting and origination by Tempus Publishing Limited.
Printed in Great Britain.

Contents

Acknowledgements

I am indebted to Belper Historical Society and Andrew Huskinson, from whose collections the majority of these photographs are drawn. This book would have been impossible to compile without their contributions of rare photographs, some of them virtually unseen until now. I am also deeply grateful to Mary Smedley, Keith Bird, Elaine Barton, Jean Bellaby, Ruth Sharpe and the staff of Belper Library, Mrs Boot, Jeanne Crane, Jean Giles, Sandra Parkin, Philip Robinson, Joyce and Randall Sanders and Phil and Cyn Varney, who all contributed photographs. Thanks go to them, and to Audrey Barrass, with whom I spent several days studying the historical society photographic collection, and who offered valuable suggestions and advice. I am grateful too for the help from Audrey, Heather Eaton, Mary Smedley, Pam Maskery, Isla Macneal and especially my ever-patient and understanding wife Mary, in reading and correcting the material written for this book – any errors that may have slipped through this net are purely my own. Thanks must also go to Brian Rich and the Duffield Frith Group for helping me to understand and appreciate some of the area's earlier history. I'd also like to thank all those, past and present, who have recorded in print the town's history. Belper is and was a fascinating place, unusual in so many ways. It is important that future generations have an opportunity to learn this, as I and so many others have in the past.

Introduction

When the Derwent Valley Mills site – stretching from Derby's Silk Mill in the south, to Matlock Bath's Masson Mills in the north – was awarded World Heritage Status in December 2001, Belper became the only town in the East Midlands to hold this significant title.

It was acknowledgement of both Belper and Milford's outstanding value and their contribution, with other mills along the Derwent, to world history.

Belper, and the neighbouring village of Milford, are old communities which have enjoyed a vibrant and fascinating development, particularly under the mill-building Strutt family during the late eighteenth and nineteenth centuries.

But their stories begin so much earlier – people had lived on these sites before the Domesday Book was recorded in 1086 (although Milford was said to be uninhabited at the time). Belper was once the Anglo-Saxon settlement of Bradelei (or Bradley), meaning Broad Clearing, but was renamed by the Normans in the early fourteenth century, becoming Beaurepaire (Beautiful Retreat) – a name that would eventually transform into Belper.

For supporting William the Conqueror in his 1066 invasion of England, Henry de Ferrers was given many lands in the Midlands. These lands included a hunting forest known as the Duffield Frith, of which the small communities of Belper and Milford were a part. At Belper he created a deer park, the smallest of eight in the Frith, where pregnant deer were cared for, or deer stored like a living larder, whilst hunting was carried out in the other parks. The deer park, with the rest of the Frith, eventually passed to the Earls (later Dukes) of Lancaster from 1267, and then to the Crown from 1399. In the seventeenth century the lands were sold off by King Charles I, but it is still possible to walk the deer park boundary today.

Both communities centred on important crossing places for the River Derwent, with a ford at Milford (as its name suggests) and a bridge at Belper. The present bridge replaced an earlier structure first mentioned in 1387, which is said to have featured the coat of arms of John O'Gaunt, Duke of Lancaster, who owned the Frith from 1359 to 1399.

It was in the last quarter of the eighteenth century that great changes came to Belper and Milford, transforming them forever. In 1775, work began on Jedediah Strutt's first mill – Strutt had given financial support to Richard Arkwright's proposals for a water-powered cotton mill in Cromford, and he now began building his own, producing fine cotton thread for his hosiery businesses.

As well as a series of mills built in Belper, Jedediah began building mills in Milford from 1780. It was the need for millworkers that provided the next major developments for the two communities, swelling the population of both. The Strutts completely recreated their surroundings to suit their needs and provide facilities for the thousands who worked for them. They began building houses, and acquiring others, so they could attract people to come and live in their mill communities, for a reasonable rent. They created farms to provide produce, a schoolroom in the North Mill attic and the Unitarian Chapel nearby, to ensure their workers were well-fed, reasonably educated and their souls saved from damnation.

The next stage of industrialisation swept through the Derwent Valley in 1838, as work started on a railway designed by the pioneering George Stephenson. About 1,500 navvies were brought in to build the line, only eight years after the world's first passenger railway – from Liverpool to Manchester – had opened. At Milford, they created the tunnel, with its impressive stone entrances. Belper was sliced in two by a deep cutting. This mile-long swathe through the heart of the town was lined with stone, and eleven bridges built so that the roads were unaffected.

As the nineteenth century progressed, the Strutts continued to shape the two communities, with more housing and schools, reading rooms, an Anglican church, even a water supply.

Belper became a hub of industry at this time, as hosiery giants Wards and their partner and later rival George Brettle flourished. Chevened, or hand-embroidered, stockings were much sought-after – even Queen Victoria herself wore hosiery created in the town.

Fortunes changed as the nineteenth century came to a close. The rest of the world had begun to compete with Britain and its industrial monopolies slipped away. In Belper, this resulted in the sale of the Strutts' business, and of the mill sites as a new century dawned. But before he sold the mills, George Herbert Strutt built the Jubilee Clock Tower, a magnificent edifice which topped the West Mill, as a celebration of Queen Victoria's long reign. And sale of the site allowed him to provide more facilities for the two communities – a church at Milford, a school, two swimming baths and the picturesque River Gardens in Belper.

In 1911, work began on Belper's biggest building, the East Mill – a cathedral to industrialisation which dominated its predecessors and became one of the Belper area's most recognisable landmarks.

Changes came again in the second half of the 20th century and both Belper and Milford lost some familiar sights as redevelopment took place. The Round Mill, then the Jubilee Clock Tower, Miss Calder's School, the mill chimney, and at Milford the mills themselves, were all demolished.

Yet enough has survived in both communities for us to still see the legacy of the Strutts, and appreciate our rich heritage, from deer parks to mills, chapels to schools, and understand why Belper and Milford lie at the centre of this World Heritage Site. And although the buildings and landscape are an important part of these communities, it is of course the people who make them come alive, something the residents of Belper and Milford have done so well. They have shown, time and again, how to celebrate both national and local events; how to entertain themselves with stage and cinema shows, carnivals and sports; and how to organise and co-ordinate groups for socialising and having fun. It is this sense of enjoyment that will hopefully be reflected in scenes of town and village life on the following pages.

Adrian Farmer
July 2004

one

Memorable
Moments

Marches through the town were sure to attract a crowd in the nineteenth century. Here, a Friendly Society demonstration through Belper in 1875 saw a huge banner held high along King Street, accompanied by a marching band. The warehouse-like building on the left was later replaced by the impressive stone-columned bank still standing on the Bridge Street corner today.

In 1892, Belper Horse Society was formed, holding its annual show in August. This comprised of trotting races and jumping, as seen here at one of the first. The show was held each year on Salt's Meadow, down Derwent Street.

A century has passed since these boys gathered around a stall at Belper fair in The Coppice, which is now the car park at the rear of the Market Place. Traditionally held in The Coppice on the weekend nearest to 31 October, the fair has been a major part of the town calendar for well over a century. One booth in 1908 boasted a giant rat. On one occasion, when it was unveiled and the cage found to be empty, there was a mad rush for the exit!

The rifle saloon belonging to A. Hall attracted a number of Victorian gentlemen from the town during this Belper fair. It was traditional in the nineteenth century for people to whitewash stone posts, wall corners and gable ends before fair week, so fair-goers could find their way home at night. Even during the First World War, the fair continued each year bar 1916. When it returned in 1917 it had shaded lights and canvassed roundabouts as well as a practised method of clearing the Coppice in case of an air raid.

For the first time since 1877, the circus arrived in Belper during October 1898. Processions took place around the town before performances, to drum up interest in the circus, and owner Lord George Sanger rode with his wife at the head. Here, some of the caged animals pass through the Market Place. Some of the best viewing places were from Compton House (now a Chinese takeaway). It would be 1912 before a fair returned again.

Huddled around the ticket office for Barnum and Bailey's Greatest Show on Earth is a crowd of circus-goers on Salt's Meadow in 1877.

The Prince of Wales's obsession with the new motorcar quickly made it a popular accessory for monied gentlemen in the late 1890s. It wasn't long before they realised the potential for racing, and here the *Daily Mail's* London to Manchester race passes the entrance to Babington Hospital on Derby Road. The Prince, later King Edward VII, was the first royal to be driven through the town, on his way to Chatsworth.

More motorcars competing in the *Daily Mail* London to Manchester Race. The wall on the far left was demolished in 1908 for work to begin on the construction of Herbert Strutt School, which opened the following year. The houses on the left were later demolished to allow for the school's expansion.

Crowds turned out on August 10 1905, to see the arrival in Belper of General William Booth, founder of the Salvation Army. The son of a Belper man, he stayed overnight at Quarry Bank (later to become St Elizabeth's Convent) after speaking at a meeting in the public hall on King Street.

From 1923, occasional celebrations were held in the town to raise money for the newly-formed League of Nations, with carnival floats, a cycle parade and concerts in the River Gardens, the shilling entry fee going to league funds. Here, employees from the English Sewing Cotton Company are dressed in national costumes from around the world, with Britannia centre stage.

Belper's Peace Celebrations – part of a national day of festivities on Saturday 19 July 1919 – began at 8.00 a.m. on the meadows by the river, with a gun salute.

Sunday school children enjoyed an afternoon singing hymns in The Parks for the 1919 Peace Celebrations. Afterwards, they all headed off in procession back to their individual churches to enjoy a celebration tea, paid for by public subscription, including these from Christ Church and the Baptist church. The flags of Britain's First World War allies flew from the Palace Cinema (right).

In January 1922, work started in Strutt Street on a building for the Belper branch of the British Legion. It was erected at the expense of George Herbert Strutt who wanted to give the 400 members somewhere to meet. It was the first building in the King Street area to be fitted with electricity. George Herbert Strutt, in the top hat, is watching General Sir Reginald Hoskins officially open the building on 25 November 1922.

The carnivals of the 1930s were held to raise funds for Derbyshire hospitals and the Belper Nursing Association. They were held in mid-July every year from 1930 to 1939, and featured many fancy-dress entrants, floats and decorated vehicles, including these on Bridge Street.

Belper Beaurythmics marching band enters the showground on Christchurch meadows for the 1951 carnival. The band, originally formed in 1935, had disbanded at the start of the Second World War. The re-launch in 1946 saw these distinctive red and white uniforms become a familiar sight in the town and at many marching competitions around the region.

After the war years, carnivals returned to the town. The British Legion organised the 1951 carnival, which again saw decorated floats and fancy dress in procession. Here a decorated lorry pauses outside the White Swan on the Market Place.

Large crowds were guaranteed for the carnivals, as can be seen here in the Market Place in 1951.

Bowling was a popular part of the carnival and wakes day events during the 1950s. Behind, the now-demolished South Mill and mill chimney are still standing in front of the East Mill.

There was always a good turnout for the Belper Wakes, although by the late 1950s, there was no longer a marquee providing teas for the children, after food was thrown at helpers and the marquee split with a knife in 1954. Subsequent years saw vouchers being distributed to children for the food vendors on the field.

Schoolchildren show their skills with the vaulting horse on the meadows during a Belper Wakes Day in the 1950s. The wakes were held on the first Monday in July with free teas for Sunday school scholars. Track events and other activities for children were followed by similar events for adults in the evening.

Above: More fun at the carnival during the 1950s – this time on the swingboats. The Jubilee Clock enabled visitors to keep an eye on the time. At 4.55 p.m. it was nearly time to go home. The clock was greatly missed when it was demolished in 1962.

Left: There were plenty of floats for this Belper Carnival procession up Belper's King Street, held during the 1980s. The photograph is taken from the window of the Belper News office, which was above the Bank of Scotland at that time.

For several years in the 1980s, a mini-marathon was held in Belper. Here the runners get off to a mass start from Belper Sports Centre in October 1983. That year's event raised £3,000 for the Caivtron Laser Appeal, and a Belper runner, David Cooper, won the event for the first time in 28 minutes and 15 seconds. The events were organised by John Bramley and Arthur Chapman, who was owner of the *Belper News*.

An annual event in the early 1990s was the barrel push up High Pavement. In June 1991, the second push took place, drawing a large crowd. The event was organised by Dick Green from the Nag's Head pub.

A new landmark for Milford was unveiled in May 1995 – a stone sculpture for the triangle of land opposite the Strutt Arms. The newly-appointed Mayor of Belper Councillor Joyce Sanders (back right) joined MEP Arlene McCarthy (back centre) and sculptor Anne Aldred (front right) for the ceremony. Unveiling of the sculpture, featuring a swan and waterwheel, had been delayed three weeks because the concrete base wasn't ready for the village May Day celebrations.

In August 1995, the River Gardens were the venue in a major celebration for the 50th anniversary of VJ Day. These three youngsters, Eloise Hallsworth-Burman, Ellen Collis and Kimberley Rice were flying the flag on the day. Entertainers included the Belper Operatic Society and singing trio Catta Chewed Ya New Shoes.

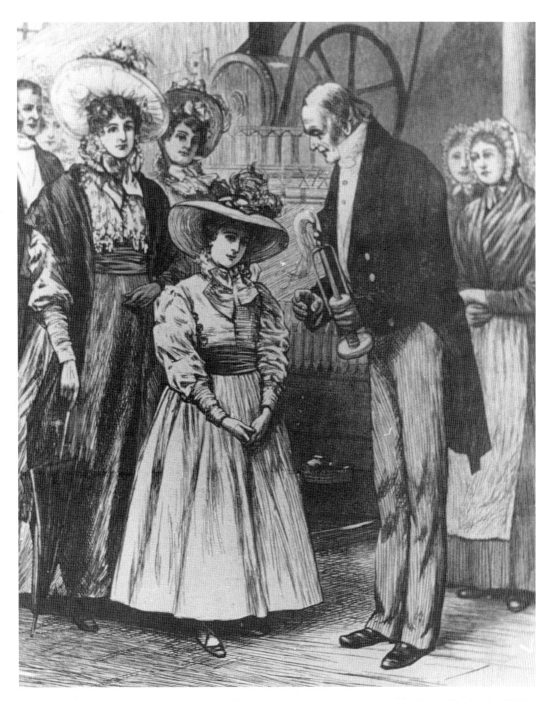

Once, the Belper area had been visited by royalty when kings and courtiers hunted in the Duffield Frith, a hunting forest of which Belper was a part. In November 1832, another royal visitor came to town, but for a very different reason. The heir to the throne was visiting Belper as part of an extended tour of the country. Princess Victoria, then just thirteen years old, inspected the Belper mills with her mother the Duchess of Kent. George Benson Strutt (right) conducted the tour before hosting lunch for the royal party at his home, Bridge Hill House.

The photographer did well to catch so many people's attention when the crowds met in Belper Market Place to celebrate Queen Victoria's Golden Jubilee in July 1887. Over 3,500 people crowded around the raised platform where the Belper United Brass Band and Milford Volunteer Band played during the singing of eight hymns.

For Victoria's Diamond Jubilee on 22 June 1897, crowds gathered again in the Market Place for a 2 p.m. celebration. Sunday schools from each of the Belper churches and chapels were allotted spaces, and each had flags and banners unfurled for the event. As in 1887, the diamond jubilee celebration saw the erection of a huge platform outside Loverock's shop (now the off-licence). On this were gathered many of the great and good of the time, including several Strutts. Mr J.B. Gough conducted the singing from the podium, and is seen addressing George Herbert Strutt.

Beacons have been lit to commemorate major celebrations (and give warning in national emergencies) for centuries. On the occasion of Queen Victoria's Diamond Jubilee in June 1897, a beacon was built on Firestone Hill, overlooking the town from the Chevin. It attracted visitors even before darkness fell and was one of about sixty that could be seen from Alport Heights, where fifty-seven Belper people finished the day, arriving by wagonette.

Amongst the celebrations for Queen Victoria's Diamond Jubilee was a gala at Salt's Meadow, on Derwent Street, with sports events and dancing accompanied by the Belper bandsmen. Even a hot air balloon could be seen on the field.

For the 1897 jubilee, the residents of Bridge Street erected a street dressing, which stood at the junction with Field Lane. This was the contribution of Mr Holden, who owned the furniture manufacturers on the left, which was later destroyed by fire in January 1905.

Belper's street dressings became grander and grander as the nineteenth century progressed – this one outside the George public house on Bridge Street in the 1890s is almost as high as the surrounding buildings.

A Market Place assembly for George V's jubilee celebrations on 6 May 1935 attracted 2,716 schoolchildren and over 2,000 adults, who were accompanied for hymns and patriotic songs by the Belper United Prize Band and the Salvation Army Band. Maypoles had been erected for the event.

Quarry House, off Chesterfield Road, won the first prize of £1 in a decorated house competition held for the coronation of King George V and Queen Mary on 22 June 1911. Joiner William Stone is pictured with (back) daughters Emmie and Gladys, family friend Fanny Beastall and his sister and housekeeper Emmie, and (front) Elsie, Doris and Maggie.

In December 1935, the Duke of Kent (centre) visited Belper to inspect the new Social Service Centre in the old courtroom on the Market Place. Thousands turned out to see him arrive, and the town was decorated with flags and bunting. At the entrance to the centre, the Duke was met by 500 children from the town's schools. Before his departure he was presented with a baby's chair made by the unemployed men who used the centre's woodwork shop.

Long Row residents were renowned for pulling out all the stops for a celebration, winning best decorated street for this, the coronation of George VI in 1937, and again in 1953.

For Queen Elizabeth II's coronation celebrations on June 2 1953, the Royal British Legion building on Strutt Street was decked out in red, white and blue. Many employers illuminated their buildings that evening, with Park Foundry said to be the most impressive.

There were a host of street parties around the town in 1981, celebrating the wedding of Prince Charles and Lady Diana Spencer. On Dovedale Crescent, they had their own royal couple dressed for the event!

Children from Pottery School met Princess Anne in November 1988. She was in the town to visit the Aristoc factory on Spencer Road, then visited the school as a thank-you to children who raised money for the Save the Children Fund.

Princess Diana spent a day in Belper on 28 April 1992. During a visit to the Whitemoor Centre, she watched a performance by the centre's drama and dance groups, although *Belper News* photographer Keith Bird caught the moment she glanced across at him. After the performance, Diana was driven to King Street where she met crowds of well-wishers.

Not all events in Belper are a success. Belper Civic Association held an exhibition over three evenings in December 1967, highlighting the progress made on projects in the town and plans for the future. Plans for the four-year-old society included a £500 landscaping scheme for St John's Chapel grounds, being studied here by association members. But sadly, only forty people turned out over the three days.

Belper has had its fair share of tragedies, as well as happy events. William Holden's furniture factory on the Bridge Street junction with Field Lane was gutted by fire on January 15, 1905. It caused £7,000 worth of damage, and a further £500 for Mr W. Walker's shop next door. The poor water supply for fire-fighters was blamed for the extent of the damage. A heavy snowfall followed the blaze, creating this bizarre landscape.

The sharp bend at Milford Bridge has caused several accidents, particularly before widening took place and the toll house was partially removed in 1906. Even here, in April 1919, a lorry careered through the bridge wall and was left dangling over the water. In May 1945 an American army lorry crashed through in almost the same spot. This time it was only the trailer behind which stopped the lorry plummeting into the water. The driver and passenger fell into the water, and had to swim for shore.

The charred remains of a Jaguar car were all that remained after fire swept through the Lion Garage in March 1966. Luckily, the forecourt was not affected. The Unity Mill chimney can be seen beyond.

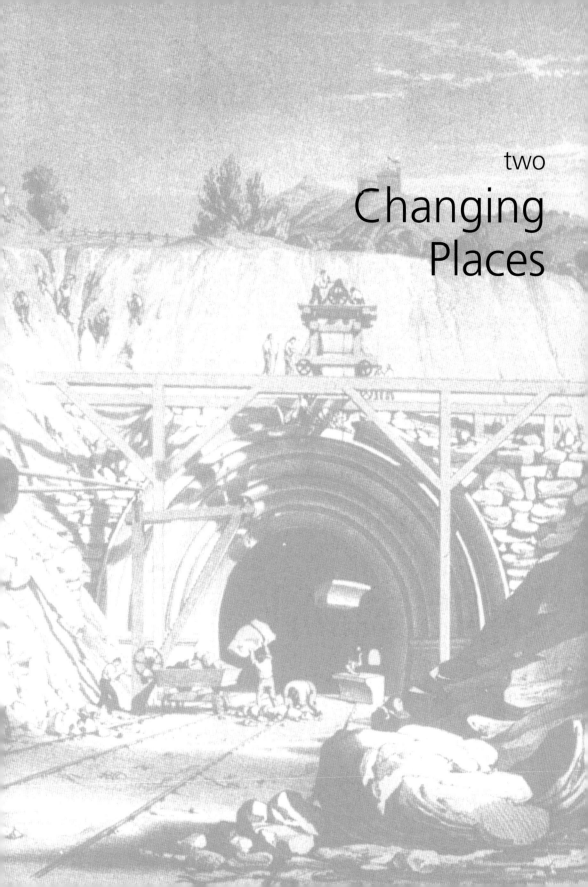

two

Changing
Places

Although many parts of Belper have changed greatly over the years, the Market Place is recognisable here, even if the transport is now very different. This horse and carriage passed through the Market Place after a heavy fall of snow in the winter of 1898/9. There were no motor vehicles in the town at this time, so this level of snow clearance was quite sufficient at the time. The Market Place was owned by the Lord of the Manor until 1953, when it was bought with the rights to hold a fair, by Belper Urban District Council for £5,000.

People gather on Belper Market Place in the late nineteenth century. It has been claimed this was not the site of Belper's original market – this was originally held off King Street, on land now occupied by the Memorial Gardens. It is said the Market Place was moved to its present site by Jedediah Strutt II, who, after his marriage to Susannah Walker in 1810, built Green Hall on King Street, but didn't want to look at traders from his front window.

A large gathering in the Market Place at the close of the nineteenth century. The site was well-used by political speakers and others. It is said that preacher John Wesley once preached here. At the rear is a mobile hoarding on a cart, advertising cigarettes. From 1909, Belper Town Band started holding concerts in the Market Place – the first, in June, was successful despite a gang of boys who tried to drown them out.

Whilst Belper Urban District Council argued over where to put Belper's permanent war memorial (until 1921!), a temporary structure was built in the market place in time for the first Remembrance Day service on November 1919.

People had complained about the tatty state of the Angel Inn – the old thatched public house in Belper Market Place – since the turn of the century. In 1896 suggestions were made for it to be demolished and a market hall built. Finally, in July 1925, it was pulled down and the site cleared. It was replaced by a Salvation Army Hall, which opened in July 1935.

A horse and carriage trots down High Street, past the Lander Lane junction, in 1909. The houses on the far left were later demolished.

Horses for sale on The Butts in October 1899, at the start of fair week. The Butts was also used for the hiring of farm workers each year at the statutes fair. This long-held tradition was ended by the outbreak of the First World War in 1914.

Before the sale of livestock moved to the land between King Street and Field Lane in 1904, sheep could be bought at market on The Butts, which was often filled to capacity with small pens for the animals.

Residents celebrate the wakes on Belper's Butts in 1875. Street dressings line the path to St John's Chapel (on the far right). The corner building, the Park Tavern, left only a narrow access in to Lander Lane.

In October 1970, the highways authority stepped in to improve the junction, and the Park Tavern was taken down to make room for a wider access to Lander Lane.

Young cricketers gather by the wooden bridge in The Parks at the end of the nineteenth century. There were far fewer trees in The Parks than there are today. Even then, rubbish was being dumped in the brook. The Parks was once the smallest deer park in the Duffield Frith, a hunting forest.

The deer had vanished from The Parks by the time a survey was carried out in 1581, and within a century the land had been sold by the king and was being farmed. From that time cows became a familiar sight, although these too disappeared in the latter half of the twentieth century.

Although no deer have roamed in The Parks at Belper for over 400 years, it has retained its boundary, and for many years was farmland. The area around the Coppice Brook and bridge has changed drastically. Looking west today there's a mass of trees obscuring the view, and the brook runs down a narrow gulley. A century ago, there were fewer trees, and wide banks to sit on. Manor Farm can be seen to the right.

A children's party in The Parks, around the time of the First World War. The bridge in the foreground runs parallel with The Fleet, but can hardly be seen for foliage now. The Coppice and The Butts can be seen in the distance.

Parkside was once a row of houses on one side of the road only. Still visible at the end of the nineteenth century was the slang, a strip of land which traditionally separated deer parks from a road, and was later taken for housing. A water gate is fitted across the Coppice Brook to prevent animals from escaping – these were used from the earliest days of the Duffield Frith, dating back to the twelfth century. On the right of the horizon is Park Mount, then home to the Smedley family, and later part of the Blounts hosiery business. At the front on the right is all that remained of Lady Well – once The Parks' greatest attraction, for providing the best water for making tea, it was demolished and plugged in 1886, and now contributes to the local water company's supplies.

Early in 1905 George Herbert Strutt gave permission for the Belper Boating Association to use the osier beds north of the mills to build a boat shed and use the waters for boating. The first seven boats took to the water on 7 May that year. There were many soggy ankles that first year as the water's edge was ill-defined for alighting boatmen and spectators alike.

The first season for the River Gardens in 1906 was so successful it was decided to make improvements at the end of the year. A central section was cleared and a bandstand added – the base can be seen here before building began in November. On 1 December a loose board hit foreman Mr R. Gray and he suffered severe head injuries, delaying the work.

A boy stands on the decking at the River Gardens to watch the Belper Boating Association's boats. The North Mill and Jubilee Clock Tower can be seen to the left. The BBA's largest boat can be seen in use on the right – this could take over twenty people at a time, but did sit rather low in the water when full!

A wooden ramp with rustic handrail of intertwined branches greeted visitors to the River Gardens as they arrived after the improvements of 1906. For special events, the shilling entry fee was paid at the entrance on Matlock Road before stepping down the ramp to see the splendour of the gardens.

The osier beds were transformed into a formal water garden in the early months of 1906, and the boat shed moved to its present site, closer to the mills. In its place the boating association built the Swiss Tea Rooms, which were thatched in heather, as a tribute to the crofts on George Herbert Strutt's Scottish estate. Sadly, the wrong methods were used and considerable leakage occurred on rainy days.

The pristine interior of the Swiss Tea Rooms, shortly after the 1906 opening. Teas, cakes and ice cream were served in here until 1961, when decreasing use and rising maintenance costs were blamed for the closure of the tea rooms by the English Sewing Cotton Company, owners of the site since 1918.

One of the harshest winters on record hit Belper hard in January 1963, with the Derwent frozen over by the River Gardens, which received a heavy coating of snow. By 24 January, the Belper weir basin had not only frozen over, but snow had settled on the solid ice, allowing the photographer to take this unusual shot from the basin itself.

The pavilion was the final addition to the River Gardens. Completed in 1908, it then had to go through alterations in 1911 to provide room for the building of the East Mill behind it. A popular public venue – and the mill-workers' canteen after the site was sold to the English Sewing Cotton Company after the First World War – it was finally demolished in November 1965. A new canteen had been built close to the North Mill earlier in the year.

The North Midland Railway, which passes through Belper and Milford, was built between 1838 and 1840, and engineered by George Stephenson. The Milford Tunnel was completed in 1839 – the work in progress was recorded in a lithograph by Samuel Russell at the request of the architect, Francis Thompson. The cost of the line had stretched the railway company so much it couldn't afford to commission the work itself. One reason for the higher than expected costs was the mile-long road cutting through Belper, lined in gritstone and featuring eleven bridges for roads. The sighting tower can be seen on the hillside above the tunnel and helped with its construction.

When the North Midland Railway opened its line through Belper in 1840, the original station – designed by Francis Thompson the line architect – was situated to the south of the town, where the Derby road crossed the track. Its siting was unpopular for being too far out of town, and a second station, on the present site, was opened in 1878.

Belper's second station was opened on 10 March 1878, and was easily accessible from King Street thanks to the demolition of the Malthouse Inn. Here a steam train heading north is being boarded. On the southbound platform a rockery spelling out the station's name was well-tended.

Above: By July 1973, the station footbridge had been removed and demolition of Belper's station was well in hand. The booking office site was cleared before the King Street bridge-widening took place, so that a supermarket could be built over it.

Left: Belper's windmill, painted here by S. Hawkins in 1890, was a familiar skyline landmark from about 1760. Falling into disuse, it was dismantled in 1891 and converted into a dwelling by Alfred Beresford in 1918. The turret on Windmill Lane can still be seen.

Hunters tea shop was close to The Paddock on King Street, at the end of the nineteenth century. The wall on the right would soon be demolished to allow for the building of a new road, Strutt Street. The gas lamp seen here, and all others in the town, was replaced with electrically powered lights in 1948, as a cost-cutting measure by Belper Urban District Council.

A new street was created for Belper as a new century – the twentieth – dawned. Again, it was the Strutt family who gave the land to the town. In recognition of this, it was decided in 1899 that it would be named Strutt Street. One of the first buildings to be built along this new street was a purpose-built post office, transferring from an older building on King Street.

Before the Memorial Gardens were given to the public in 1921, they were known as The Paddock, part of the grounds for Green Hall on the opposite side of King Street. The gardens were lower than they are today – the ground at the far side was raised to allow for the creation of an air raid shelter during the 1914–18 war. Two more were added at the King Street end during the Second World War. The area on the right was sold to the Dalton family so they could build an oil refinery after the First World War – this transferred to Derby Road in 1934.

It's easy to see why these Swiss-style homes were known as Ivy Cottages for many years. The decorative white edging was added by Jedediah Strutt II when he built Green Hall. As the cottages could be seen from his home, he wanted them to have the Swiss styling that was so fashionable in the earlier nineteenth century. Large hoardings were a familiar sight in the town even a century ago.

When Lieutenant Spacey returned from France on leave from the First World War in 1916, flags, bunting and umbrellas decorated the Park Foundry by his Becksitch Lane home.

After the fire of January 1905 destroyed Holden's furniture factory, the site of the gutted stables on Field Lane was sold for housing. The new row of red-brick houses, seen on the left, were soon in place – and much admired for their stylish bay windows. The dusty roads caused problems every summer – by 1910 Belper Urban District Council were looking at ways of improving road surfaces, and were keeping a watchful eye on a trial scheme using tarmac on the promenade at Brighton. This had been produced at a Denby furnace.

Painter Frank Beresford's childhood home in Belper had been Field House, which stood on the corner of Field Lane and Bridge Street until road-widening proposals saw it demolished in the 1970s. The Beresford family had a drapery business here, but a fire in 1910 saw many of Beresford's early paintings destroyed – over-zealous firemen drenched his wooden studio next to the building in their attempts to quash the flames.

Above: The building of Bessalone Reservoir – another gift to the town from the Strutt family – ensured a plentiful supply of water for the town. In 1895 George Henry Strutt offered an interest-free loan for improvements to the water supply. When he died three months later, he left instructions that the loan be cancelled, and paid for the building of the reservoir at Bessalone, off Crich Lane.

Right: The Belper Memorial Tower, to be dedicated to Belper's benefactor George Henry Strutt, was to have been built in the centre of the new Bessalone Reservoir in 1897 in thanks for George Henry's gift of water for the town. This 65 ft tower would have cost £600 but George Henry's widow refused to allow the spending of such a sum, and the tower was never erected.

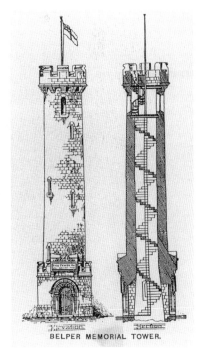

BELPER MEMORIAL TOWER.

Left: By 1967, Belper was desperately in need of better drains, and there were some major disturbances to the roads, including Mill Street, where workmen battled on in the August sunshine.

Below: In 1963 it was decided to build Belper a brand new fire station, in the shadow of the East Mill. By the end of February 1964, some of the building work had been completed, and a training tower was being erected.

Belper's main bridge, close to the mills, has been a crossing place since the time of the Duffield Frith, when the Duke of Lancaster John O'Gaunt is said to have erected a bridge to connect the two halves of his hunting forest. Work on the present bridge began in 1796 and took two years – it cost £2,200 and 5d. Here it is before widening in 1957.

The lack of leaves in the trees provides a view of the Strutt mills in 1895. Central is William Strutt's North Mill of 1804, with mill cottages in front and the chimney of 1854 behind. On the left is the cottage hospital garden, with Green Walk – an elevated pathway allowing the Strutt family easy access from their Bridge Hill home to the mills. Officially the Strutts were the only ones allowed to use it, and it was swept every Sunday morning before their weekly walk to Christ Church.

On Bridge Hill stood one of the Strutt homes, now demolished. The library of Bridge Hill House reflects the thirst for knowledge which drove the innovating Strutt family. They felt reading and writing were essential abilities for all their workers, and established schools to achieve this. On top of the facing bookcase is the bust of William, Jedediah's eldest son, who built the North Mill. This is now held by Derby Museum and Art Gallery.

The breakfast room of Bridge Hill House. Portraits of George Benson Strutt, who built the house in 1793, and his wife Catherina, are mounted on either side of the main window.

The morning room of Bridge Hill House may have been used to entertain Princess Victoria when she visited the house in 1832.

Paintings line the walls of the main staircase in Bridge Hill House. All these were sold at auction by the Strutt family when they emptied the house in December 1931, including a Gainsborough. Within months the house had been completely demolished.

The powerful Derwent has flooded its banks in Belper throughout history – in 1795 the old bridge was swept away. Here in 1907, the newly-created River Gardens and the gardens of the Talbot Inn on the opposite bank were underwater, as were these fields south of the bridge. That didn't stop these boys from turning out, fascinated by the force of the water.

On 10 December 1966, Belper was hit by one of the worst floods in living memory. The Bridgefoot area was particularly badly affected, as the Derwent burst its bank above the weir and swept over the road, causing traffic to be stranded.

A cart sits in the middle of the road at Bridgefoot – perhaps the owner is inside the urinal that then stood at the centre of the junction! The cottage hospital, run by the Strutts for the mill-workers, is almost hidden in ivy on the right. The wall on the left was the boundary for the hospital garden, which eventually became overgrown, and was transformed into a public garden, Beaurepaire, in 2004.

After many years in the centre of the road, where privacy was minimal but the smell was distant for passers-by, the Bridgefoot urinal was pulled down, and a new facility, still for men only, provided on the south side of the road. The old urinal was replaced with a horse trough, but this in turn was destroyed when a lorry collided with it in 1952.

The Talbot Hotel is one of Belper's oldest hostelries. The last major rebuilding work was carried out in 1660, when Charles II was restored to the throne and drinking once more became an acceptable form of entertainment. The Talbot dog was the emblem of the Earls of Shrewsbury, who had interests within the Duffield Frith, and may have originally owned the inn or the land on which it was built. Stretching away is Bridge Hill, part of the Ashbourne road, which was well used as a coal route in the time of the Frith.

Organised hunting has taken place in the Belper area for nearly a thousand years. Originally it was deer in the parks of the Duffield Frith. By the twentieth century it was foxes – this meet started from the Bull's Head on Belper Lane End shortly after the First World War.

Bridge House School, run by the Misses Calder, stood in the shadow of the South Mill, and it was said you could hear the mill machinery from the classrooms. Children and staff are seen here at the start of the twentieth century. The school was demolished, with the South Mill, in 1962.

In almost all photographs of the mills and Triangle area taken before 1960, the great tree outside the school of the Misses Calder can be clearly seen. When the decision came to demolish the school, and the neighbouring South Mill, it meant the tree also had to go. Stripped of its branches, the trunk was finally pulled down before work began on the buildings in 1962.

This was the new Parks Secondary Modern School, when it opened in 1955. The uniform was a maroon blazer with blue piping and a matching cap for the boys and beret for the girls. The first head boy was Desmond Hodgkinson and the first head girl Pauline Wathall. The school was eventually amalgamated with the new Belper High School, and in July 1991 the Parks site was closed altogether, despite many complaints from parents. The school was then demolished. A planning application to build a new primary school, and a mass of housing, on the site was considered by Amber Valley Borough Council in 2004.

Belper's present library was opened in June 1937. Previously, it had been called The Hollies, home of Dr and Mrs Heyworth. This is the Hunter Room in the spring of 1938, containing a collection of books donated from the late Colonel Hunter's personal library. In 2004, Derbyshire County Council announced plans to replace the library with a new purpose-built building.

Belper's oldest building is St John's Chapel – by the time this photograph was taken in 1872 it was already over 600 years old. Originally dedicated to St Thomas, it became St John's during Henry VIII's sweeping Reformation to distance the chapel from the anti-royalist Thomas Becket. At this time, the two yews by the Butts entrance were the only trees in the chapel yard, giving a clear view of St Peter's from Chapel Hollow (later to be renamed St John's Road) .

The ancient yew trees which stood in the grounds of St John's Chapel eventually became unsafe, one being topped in 1880 and later cut down, the second blown down in the fierce gale of November 1911. The gates were replaced with a lychgate given during 1922 in memory of Isaac and Elizabeth Jane Hanson, as part of a renovation scheme for the chapel that year.

Above: The interior of St John's Chapel in 1920, before the £1,000 renovation scheme began in 1922 to restore its former glory. Old plaster was chipped away, the aisle covered, the pews replaced and the font, seen on the right, crossed the aisle to stand by the vestry door.

Left: A nineteenth century view of St Peter's church, before the trees began to hide it. Work began on the church in 1822 and it was consecrated in 1824.

After a fire in the tower of St Peter's church in March 1949, one of its four pinnacles was badly damaged. When scaffolding was erected and a closer inspection made, it was realised that the problem was even more extensive than anticipated. Rather than carry on with an extremely costly and difficult repair programme, all four pinnacles were removed from the tower. Extensive redecorating followed in October 1949 for the first time in over 25 years. It cost over £500 to achieve. Whilst work was being carried out, nearby St John's Chapel had its largest congregations of the twentieth century.

Changing fortunes and dwindling congregations resulted in the amalgamation of Methodist congregations in the 1960s, and the closure of the Salem Chapel on Green Lane and the Field Head Chapel on Chesterfield Road. When the latter (right) was demolished in the winter of 1967/68, it was preceded by the neighbouring chapel cottage.

The twentieth century had a lesser impact on Milford than it did on Belper, although the mills were demolished in the 1960s. It is still possible to see much of the community created by the Strutt family. Looking north towards Milford's Hopping Hill a century ago, many of the buildings seen here were Strutt-built to house mill-workers. The land for the church (bottom left) was donated by George Herbert Strutt. On the right are the unique back-to-back interlocking houses which form East and West Terraces.

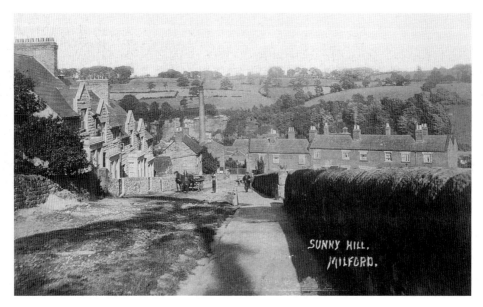

More Strutt housing on Sunny Hill, looking down towards the mill chimney. The buildings on the right are back-to-back housing bought by the Strutts in 1831 to fulfil their need for small properties for single workers. The property on the left with attic gables was built by the Strutt Estate early in the twentieth century.

The long footbridge over the Derwent near Hopping Hill, Milford, was still in use until the floods of 22 May 1932 swept it away. Hopping Hill consists mainly of Strutt-built housing – the rest was acquired for their workers.

This is a slightly later view of Hopping Hill and the foundry site by the river. The footbridge over the Derwent is partly hidden by the trees. Here the Co-op building of 1910 can be seen on the Derby road. The foundry site (left) has been well used for centuries, and was once the site of the gasworks for the Milford Mills – reputably the first of its kind in the world.

Boys enjoy a game of cricket in the former Terrace Quarry on the Derby Road at Milford, a century ago. The site was newly established as a recreation area for the village, with a bench provided!

The mill complex and bridge at Milford, shortly after the mills had been leased to the English Sewing Cotton Company in 1897. Built in 1793 to a design by William Strutt, the bridge replaced a ford. The cost of the bridge, toll house (you had to pay to cross!) and bridge over the mill watercourses cost £2,153 17s 1d. On the far left is the mill clock tower.

The original Milford suspension bridge in 1911. Opening in 1826, the same year as the world's first suspension bridge, it is said to have influenced the construction of Brunel's Clifton suspension bridge at Bristol in 1864. Designed by William Strutt to replace a notoriously dangerous ford, it was demolished in 1946 and a new bridge was erected in 1982.

The original footbridge over the Derwent at Milford, with the old flour mill on the left – this is now part of a garden centre.

The junction by the Strutt Arms in Milford has changed little over the past century, although the road was much narrower as it turned right behind the public house, past the mills to cross the river bridge. Just visible along the Chevin road is Milford School, provided by the Strutts for the mill children.

Bank Buildings (later Banks Buildings) run along the Chevin road, west of the river. These too were provided by the Strutt family for their workers. Originally built in 1792, they were demolished and rebuilt c.1910 to their present design.

three

Belper's People

Schooling has changed greatly in Belper since the Strutts opened their schoolroom in the attic space of the North Mill. Here, Miss Elsie Kirk was the teacher in this classroom scene at High Street Infants School in 1912. Sitting under the third picture is Elsie Stone, with Nellie Maskery sitting beside her. The school was closed in 1973 during a major re-organisation of the education system, and it was later demolished.

Students from Belper's National School – later called St John's – line up in The Coppice, c. 1900. The school itself stood on The Butts, by the chapel. The Manor Farm and outbuildings can be seen behind.

Boys from St John's School gather in the school yard behind the neighbouring chapel for a very serious contest during an autumn term in the 1930s. It was most boys' dream to be a conkering hero!

Maypole dancing is still a valued tradition in Milford today, performed around the village as part of an annual procession and finishing in the school playground. Here it took place inside Milford School, during the 1940s. The school was built by the Strutt family to help in the education of the workforce.

These girls from Long Row School swam to success in 1961, winning a trophy for their skills in the pool. Elaine Ryde is holding the winning shield. The teacher with them is Miss Barlow.

Boys from another Strutt-built school, Long Row, line up for the school photographer in Coronation year, 1953.

Children from St John's School gather in the neighbouring chapel for a harvest celebration in the 1950s. Headmaster Harold Whitworth cared greatly for the chapel which shared its name with his school. He ensured that it was well-used by the school even when forgotten by others during much of the twentieth century.

St John's headmaster Harold Whitworth teaches music to children, including Patsy Timms (second right), in the chapel grounds during the 1950s.

Left: An annual event at St John's School when it stood on The Butts was a nativity in the chapel. This from the early 1950s features Christine Elliott as one of the angels.

Below: A guard of honour met Colonel G.W. Parsons when he came to Herbert Strutt School in May 1967 to inspect the school's army cadets. Nearly seventy cadets took part in the day's events, which included a demonstration on how to ambush and a leadership exercise in getting a large heavy box over a 20ft high wall and across a stream. The latter was won by Corporal P. Saunders and his team.

A march against hunger by fifteen-year-old Herbert Strutt schoolgirl Wendy Christy helped raise funds for a special Land Rover to be sent to Nigeria to help educate farmers about efficiency. With sponsors including Belper MP George Brown, Wendy set off on 5 March, 1966, walking part of an official route through Derbyshire. The Land Rover visited Pottery School before heading out for Nigeria later in the year.

Over 100 people turned out for the Christmas nativity held at St Elizabeth's School in December 1971, including the Mayor and Mayoress of Derby. In all, one hundred children took part from the infant classes. The nativity was followed by another production, *Christmas Phantasy*, provided by the junior classes.

A Resounding Tinkle was the name of the Herbert Strutt School play performed by students in November 1971. Producer Mr H. Thomas, the school's economics master, described it as a work from the theatre of the absurd. Amongst the cast were Ralph Castledine, Chris Harrison, John Slaney, Tim Blackshaw, Robert Hislop, Mavis Pugson, Chris Marriott, Jane Fransham, Alison Sealey, Jonathan Gregory, Donald McKee, David Wilkins, David Mellor, Rosie Wilby, Carol Gaunt, Helen Dickie and Tim Burkinshaw.

The summer term of 1991 ended in a feast of fun for pupils. There were lots of food-related games and quizzes to play, including a jelly on a spoon race and a tossing the oatcake contest. Here, children prepare to race with a plate full of beans.

The church has played an important part of Belper life ever since St John's was built in the thirteenth century. This group of Victorian churchmen were in relaxed mood by the main door of St Peter's church, at the end of the nineteenth century. Of those standing at the rear, William Stone is third and Charles Kirk fourth from left. Standing at the front right is Robert Stone, then proprietor of the Duke of Devonshire public house on Bridge Street.

A Sunday school anniversary for Field Head Primitive Methodist Chapel on Chesterfield Road, held, ironically, outside the Queen's Head public house. The anniversary was held on the third Sunday in June every year from 1824, and featured a procession around the town with hymns sung at certain points.

These were the workmen who built St Swithun's church in 1912/13. A rapid population growth in the Holbrook Road area of the town at the end of the nineteenth century and start of the twentieth necessitated the need for the new mission church, a satellite of St Peter's.

A dedication ceremony for St Swithun's church, led by the Bishop of Derby, was held on 30 April 1913. This included a walk around the outside of the church for clergy and the choir, seen here under the watchful eye of the local bobby. After the ceremony, a reception was held at the home of Mrs Hanson of The Mount, Belper – it was her money alone that had paid for the church, in memory of her husband, a director at George Brettle and Co.

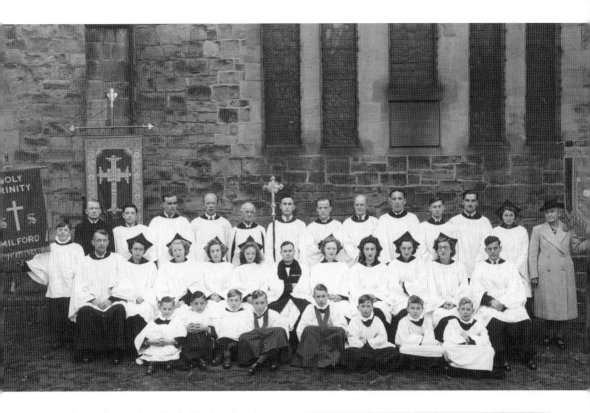

Above: The choir of Holy Trinity church, Milford, *c.* 1948. They are, from left to right, back row: David Broomhead; verger Reg Waldron; Ken Woodhead; Norman Mellor; Noel Bowmer; organist Harry Kirk; crucifer Arthur Bellaby; Walter Christan; Charlie Walker; Harold Bellaby; John Orme; Ralph Gell; Clarice Eley and Mrs A. Hunt, middle row: choirmaster Harry Merrifield; Margaret Greatorex; Audrey Barr; June Walker; Dorothy Knifton; the Revd Harold Morgan; Molly Knifton; Mary Bellaby; Jean Pedley; Betty Bellaby and Albert Spencer, front row: Tony Beard, Ivan Beeston, Bryan Orme, Trevor Walker, David Merrifield, John Eastgate, David ? and Michael Merrifield.

Right: These choirboys posed outside Milford's Holy Trinity church in 1953, for the church's 1954 calendar. The boys are, from left to right: David Pickard; Peter Makin; Phillip Flanders and David Varney.

Children were dressed in their best for the annual patronal walk and festival for St Peter's church in the 1950s. From King Street they processed to St Peter's for the service.

Sunday school girls dressed up as gypsies for a concert at Field Head Chapel on Chesterfield Road in 1958. Left to right they are: Patsy Taylor; Maureen Hackman; Judith Pickering; Margaret Kettlewell; Rayleen Poplar; Susan Worthy; Kathleen Moran; Sandra Lucking and Jane Jackson.

Belper Baptist church Sunday school held a Christmas party in 1960 for its members. That week the scholars also held a toy service, raising £6 3s for Blind Orphans in Bethlehem and donating toys to the local children's homes.

A coffee evening may sound rather grown up for the Belper Congregational church youth club in August 1966, until you realise the most popular activity was a piano-smashing competition – three pianos were destroyed in one evening!

The Belper Baptist Campaigners held a sausage sizzle event on Christchurch Meadows by the River Derwent in August 1966. The Junos also attended, and the two groups built two campfires on which to cook their supper.

About sixty parents and children turned out for a mystery evening organised by the scholars and committee of Belper Central Methodist church PTA in October 1967. Sketches, community singing, dancing and an exhibition were the mystery entertainment provided. The Revd A.E. Gibbons is talking to children who enjoyed the evening.

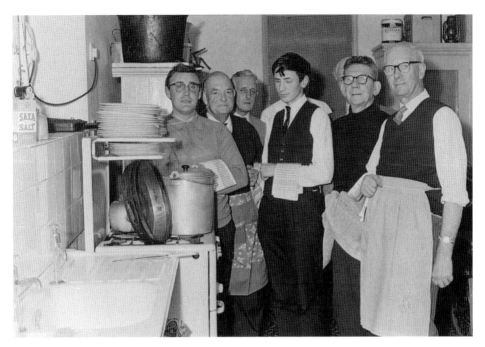

A pie and mash supper to celebrate the 1968 harvest festivities was organised by the Men's Society branch based at Christ Church. Members who cooked and served up the supper are seen here raising £11 towards funds.

Colonel Peter Hilton, County Commandant of the Cadet Force, and later Lord Lieutenant for Derbyshire, opened St Peter's church garden party in June 1966, and is seen here with Kim and Mandy Chambers at the event.

George Herbert Strutt was in charge of this parade by the Belper and Milford Volunteers in The Butts, *c.* 1890. Traditionally, drill was at 10 a.m. on a Sunday, beginning at the Market Place. In the early days of the battalion, the Revd Joseph Bradshaw would open proceedings by reading church prayers on horseback, before they moved down to the Derwent Meadows. Originally the uniform consisted of a scarlet coat, yellow collar and cuffs, and white trousers.

Belper Urban District Council's fire brigade, *c.* 1896 in the Belper mill yard. In 1909 their handcart was replaced with a steam-powered engine, funded equally by the council, George Herbert Strutt and the mill-owners, the English Sewing Cotton Company, on whose premises it was kept.

During the First World War of 1914–18, former Strutt residence Green Hall was converted into a convalescence home for injured soldiers. Here, patients and nursing staff relax in the grounds.

Members of the St John Ambulance Brigade show they're ready for war as September 1939 approached. Sandbags were stacked outside the drill hall on Cluster Road. Amongst them is Bill Rodgers (third from right in the centre row).

On 14 May 1944, Lady Mountbatten visited Belper for an inspection of the town branch of the St John Ambulance Brigade. Lady Mountbatten was superintendent–in–chief of the brigade, and is seen speaking to Sid Hunt during the inspection on Long Row.

Some of the cadets and staff from the brigade's first aid post on Long Row, before Lady Mountbatten's arrival in May 1944.

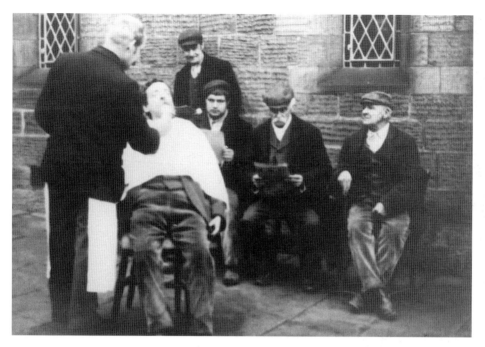

Inmates at Belper Workhouse (now Babington Hospital) prayed for fine weather when it was time for a shave and a haircut – these were regularly given outside by a visiting barber.

With their nurses and overseer are children from Belper Workhouse. It was shortly after this time, in November 1904, that mothers from the workhouse requested that the building be renamed Babington House. They were reluctant to put the word 'workhouse' on their children's birth certificates.

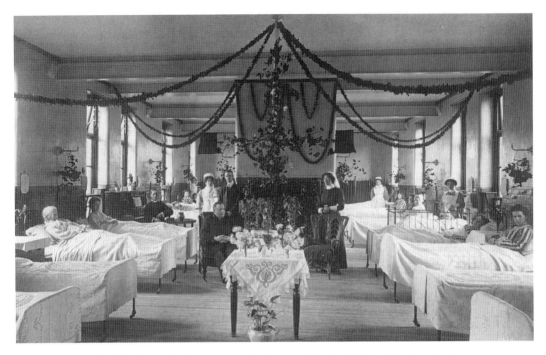

Lady patients in the Workhouse Infirmary (now Babington Hospital) join staff and a piano-playing clergy to celebrate the coronation of King George V in 1911. As well as wards decorated with foliage, inmates received a cold meat dinner and an extra ounce of tobacco as part of the celebrations. All routine work was suspended, but on the casting vote of the chairman, the workhouse governors decided not to allow the inmates any ale to celebrate.

Five-year-old Dawn Booth of Nottingham Road was crowned Belper's May Queen on the stage of the Ritz Cinema in 1966. Alderman Mrs Ada Belfield performed the crowning, and they are watched here by Ritz manager Mr H. Surples, and members of the cinema's Star Junior Club.

A team from the First Belper (Christ Church) Pack won the Belper District Cub Scouts winter competition, held at the Central Methodist Schoolroom on Chapel Street in March 1967. They received their trophy from Mr W Marsh, president of the Belper District Scout Council.

Balloons take to the air in Milford Scout group's balloon race, launched from Belper Market Place in May 1971.

Born at Christmas in 1823, Sammy Ashton started life as a Belper nailmaker but for a time was a travelling showman accompanied by birds, animals and a monkey, who were all taken by handcart to entertain at parties and private functions. Not a financial success, he returned to Belper and sold newspapers, keeping his monkey as a reminder of his colourful past. Here he is in later life, in Belper Market Place. Sammy was quite capable of turning out in a stove pipe hat and elegant clothes when the mood took him, and was also known for his quick tongue, even with Mr Strutt himself!

Jimmy Bakewell was Belper's first car owner. In the days of the horse and cart, he and his motor were a novelty attraction much marvelled at by Belper folk.

George Winn, the original owner of the *Belper News* from 1896 to 1901, wasn't shy of dressing up for special events, donning lady's clothing here to play Charley's Aunt for a late nineteenth-century carnival.

Dressed for a late Victorian carnival procession is Albert Staniforth, owner of a boot and shoe shop next to the Railway Hotel on King Street, dressed as Yankee Doodle Dandy.

Crowds gather at The Triangle to see George Herbert Strutt (with his back to the camera) award a sergeant returning from the First World War of 1914–18.

From its earliest days, the River Gardens were used as the perfect setting for large group photographs. Organisations in the town or visiting groups from further afield all gathered by the bandstand for a photograph recording of their visit.

Freezing conditions and a heavy fall of snow allowed ice-skating on the fishpond on Wyver Lane during this 1890s winter. Clearly it was a men-only activity, and bowler hats were essential! Behind them is the Wyver Lane signal box, now long gone.

Many thousands of people have worked in Belper's cotton mills since 1776, the great majority being women. By the twentieth century retired workers were able to stay in touch, with outings arranged, including one on 22 June 1968 for which this group are gathered by the North Mill.

A tramp's supper at the Fisherman's Rest, Broadholme, saw over twenty customers dressing down to raise money for the British Railways Kidney Unit Fund in May 1968. Organised by Mr and Mrs Arkell, it was judged by Wendy George, who had just come third in the Miss England contest.

The Fleet Well Dressing Group revived this ancient tradition throughout the 1960s. As well as a large dressing provided by the adults, children were encouraged to produce their own, smaller version. In 1961 this group produced this biblically-themed dressing. Amongst the children taking part were Fiona Harrison, Stephen Watson, Joan and Philip Smith and Betty Linthwaite.

Children working on the border of the group's first well dressing – entitled Moses in the Bullrushes – in the lean-to belonging to organisers Mr and Mrs Robson, in 1960.

The cast of Erminie on stage in Belper's Public Hall at the top of King Street. The popular Belper Operatic Society production ran from 21 to 25 February 1911. Tickets of 2s, 1s or 6d on the promenade raised money for local charities.

Three years later, Belper Operatic Society are seen dressed for a performance of the Yeoman of the Guard, their last production before the outbreak of war in 1914.

It's a long way from being James Bond! Timothy Dalton (third from left) was just seventeen when he donned Arabian dress to appear in *Out of the Frying Pan* with the Belper Players in 1963. This was his first appearance with the group – he went on to play the lead role in another production, *Billy Liar*.

Belper Players were providing their own entertainment for their annual dinner in January 1966. Members performed and dressed for an old time music hall at the Masonic Rooms on Campbell Street. Belper architect Mr A.P. Taylor was guest speaker. Nearly 100 members, in various costumes, attended.

Pottery School's Robin Hood theme proved a big hit with the judges at the 1991 carnival, winning first prize in the float competition. They received a trophy from town mayor Les Beardmore.

Members of Belper WI went back to school in June 1994 for their St Trinian's float in the Belper carnival. Other float entries that year were Safeway with Peter Pan, Alton Manor Nursery with Noah's Ark (joint winners with the WI) and Our Lady's church with God is Love.

The building of the new swimming baths on Gibfield Lane in 1910 encouraged a greater number of people to take up swimming as a pastime. Amongst these were the members of the Belper Swimming Club, who all proudly displayed the club's initials on their costumes. The club was for men only – the ladies used the baths at separate times, during which all male swimmers and spectators were banned!

Belper Town Football Club players take a break from intensive training in August 1968, ready for the start of a new season in the Midland League.

A first outing for the Thornton's ladies football team ended in 7-1 defeat against Brettles in March 1971. The team, seen here in stripes, were: Pat Bryant; Pat Waller; Lynda Wathall; Bridgit Taylor; Helen Edwards; Sue Lander; Sue Blount; Pat Swift; Angie Evans; Clare Fantom and Yvonne Edwards.

The Glow-Worm Sports and Social Club swept the board in 1973; winning four trophies. These were, from left to right: the Darts League Winners Shield; the Darts Cup Winners Cup; the Cricket Division Two Winners Shield and the Alfreton and District Table Tennis League Division Four Winners Cup.

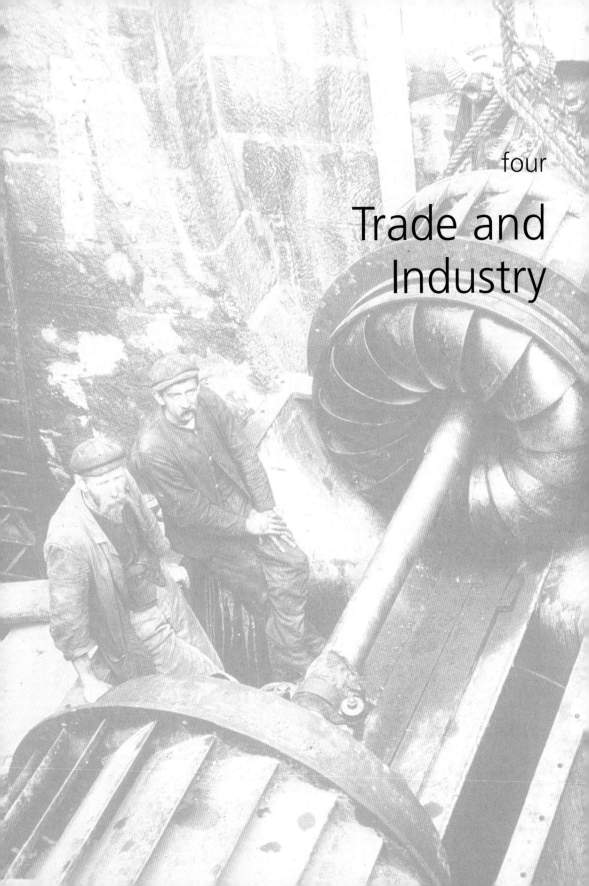

four

Trade and
Industry

One of Belper's better-known shops a century ago was Hunters Tea Stores, complete with meat joints hanging outside, and butter 1s/lb. Opening in King Street between 1895 and 1898, it was still serving the public during the Second World War.

Edward Ryde opened on Bridge Street as a butcher in the 1890s. Soon he had two shops on the same street – one near to The Triangle, and this second shop facing the King Street junction. Here in 1935 is Ethel Ryde, first wife of proprietor Charlie Ryde, in the doorway of the butcher's shop.

Waterloo House – built at the time of the victory against Napoleon – was a millinery run by the Gibson Brothers, and then John Burton in the late 1890s, until a blaze broke out destroying much of the building. Instead of rebuilding, the removal of the shop allowed for wider access from Chesterfield Road and St Peter's church into the Market Place area.

For many years, 8 Market Place was a traditional chemist's shop, with vast cellars below for the storage of bottles. Until 1927, C.W. Southern brewed and sold his own ginger beer and iron brew, in pot bottles produced by the Bourne family at Denby Pottery. From 1993, the former stables at the rear became home to the *Belper News*.

Above: A distinctive higher doorway at the side of Burkinshaw's chemist shop on Church Street. William Burkinshaw opened the shop around 1876, but by 1912 Alfred Burkinshaw was using the premises to sell electrical goods. In 1927 the business moved to the grander premises of 8 Market Place, which continued as a chemist's shop.

Right: House furnishers C.E. Goodliffe were renowned for quality goods after opening, *c.* 1927. Their Bridge Street shop with its distinctive large first floor windows still stands close to the Derwent Street junction.

In 1956 a new style of building was planned for the top of King Street, providing a massive extension to the Ripley Co-operative Society building on the Market Place.

In 1973 redevelopment saw the removal of these shops on King Street, and the railway bridge widened, in order that the new Fine Fare supermarket could be built. The precinct of shops on the left curved in to the entrance for the station. Their removal and the new building would hide the station from King Street shoppers completely.

Before the First World War the Saturday market stalls filled the Market Place – here they even block the road from High Street! Falling use and aging stalls resulted in the market being labelled 'a shanty town' by councillors in 1957. By then there were only six stalls left, and this trend would continue until the popular farmers' markets began in 2002.

Nailmaking was Belper's greatest industry before the arrival of the cotton mills. By the middle of the nineteenth century about 400 nailmakers like this man lived and worked in the town. But this had fallen to thirty-eight by 1901, thanks to the arrival of machine-made nails, and it was only a few years later that Belper's oldest industry disappeared.

A mid-nineteenth century view of the Strutt mills, with the North Mill partly hidden by trees and the West Mill topped by the gazebo which was later placed on the Jubilee Clock Tower. Behind is the town, including Belper's windmill on the horizon and the newly finished St Peter's church, dedicated in 1824.

There's more than a little 'bending' of the truth in this illustration of the Strutt mills used in advertising and trade journals in the 1870s and 1880s. To make the mills 'look their best', the windowless gable end of the North Mill has been adorned with not only windows but a porch entrance too, the cottages in the North Mill yard have been converted to shrubbery, and the town beyond has been transformed into a forest, complete with the Milford mills nestling in the background, despite being several miles down river! However, it is likely the ancillary buildings to the left did resemble the shape shown here before they were cleared for the building of the East Mill in 1911. The illustration may pre-date the building of the 1854 mill chimney.

The distinctive horseshoe weir of 1797 was built by the Strutts to provide a sufficient lagoon of water – 22 acres – to power their ever-increasing number of waterwheel-driven mills. The sluice gates on the far left were known locally as 'bezzleguts'. At one stage there were eleven wheels being fed by the water from the river Derwent. Even in this earliest-known photograph of the weir from around 1897 there are trees in the otherwise cobbled weir basin.

In 1895, shortly before the cotton-spinning business was sold on to the newly-created English Sewing Cotton Company, the Strutts commissioned photographs to be taken of all their employees. Each section of the mill staff gathered for these photographs, and their names were recorded. All these photographs still survive today in Strutt's North Mill.

The Gangway footbridge connected the mills on either side of the Ashbourne Road, following the building of the West Mill on the southern side in 1796. Gun embrasures were added in 1810, to defend the mills in case of attack from mill-wreckers, although the Strutts never suffered an attack.

The West Mill was completed in 1796, just a year before Jedediah Strutt died. Unusually, ornamentation was added to this mill in the form of a six-pillared gazebo on the roof. Clock faces were placed on the three sides closest to the road. The West Mill was reached from the road by a covered walkway over a water channel – children often stood and watched the swirling eddies below through the railings on the road.

A photographer pauses in his work by the Strutt mills in 1895. Industry on such a scale – this was for some years the world's largest mill complex in single ownership – attracted much attention in the nineteenth century. On the right is the great tree in the grounds of Bridge House School – it was nearly as tall as the mills! This is before the Jubilee Clock Tower would dominate the West Mill side of the road.

George Herbert Strutt decided in February 1897 to honour a Queen who was not only celebrating her Diamond Jubilee, but had visited the Strutt mills as a child. Queen Victoria had even received a copy of the annual Strutt mills' calendar for many, many years. He paid for this Jubilee Clock Tower out of his own pocket – a vast edifice that dominated the town. It was unveiled the following year, reusing the gazebo it replaced, which now stood on top of the tower.

A snowfall at the close of the nineteenth century made the new Jubilee Clock Tower look all the more magical. The clock was set going in October 1898. The dials were, at the time of its unveiling, the largest in Derbyshire.

In 1907, a new form of power was brought to the Milford mills. These turbines were lowered into place, providing more efficient use of the water than the old wheel. They were officially opened the following year by Mrs Strutt and her daughter. The empty pit can still be seen on the mill site.

A low river level allows a chance to see the horseshoe weir from the western bank of the Derwent. Behind, the North Mill and Jubilee Clock Tower stand proud in the days before the East Mill overshadowed them. The mill chimney of 1854 is almost hidden by the trees on the left, and close to it are the buildings which had to be demolished before the East Mill was erected.

The early stages of construction for the East Mill involved the erecting of steel 'stilts' for the building to stand over the water courses. For this work to be done the sluice gates were closed and the water courses emptied. This caused a disruption in the power for the mills, so labourers had to work seven days a week – even Sundays – to get this part of the work done.

Schoolboys and the public gathered around the North Mill water channel, and on the Handyside Bridge by the pavilion (right) to watch the East Mill's first steel 'stilts' being put into place during the first week of construction.

With the southern corner of the three-year-old pavilion (left) removed during the summer of 1911 to make enough room for the building of the East Mill, work began on the mill itself on 12 August 1911.

The steam-powered crane brought in to help with the construction of the East Mill after work began in August 1911. With 1,400 tons of steel girders and four million bricks to work with, it was kept busy in the months ahead.

The steel framework of the East Mill was starting to come together as winter approached. It was principles developed by William Strutt for the building of the iron-framed North Mill in 1804 which, taken a stage further, were used on the East Mill 107 years later.

Work carried on apace through 1912, by which time the sixth floor of the East Mill was taking shape. With no scaffolding, and flat caps instead of hard hats, it was a brave group of builders who worked on the very edge of the building.

Although the building work had been virtually completed in 1912, it wasn't until a sunny July day in 1913 that all the equipment had been fitted and the official opening of Belper's East Mill could take place. Crowds (seen here from the mill itself) gathered in the mill yard to see the powerhouse unlocked with a golden key by Mrs Morgan, wife of the chairman of the English Sewing Cotton Company, who owned the new mill. The arch at the rear of the picture was later removed – it is now the main entrance to the River Gardens.

S 11833 NEW MILL. BELPER.

The East Mill, shortly after work was completed in 1913, dwarfs the North Mill of 1804. At this time there were still cottages along the river wall.

The 1960s saw the English Sewing Cotton Company passing on many of its skills to countries around the world, keen to learn spinning manufacture and join the industrial world. It was for this reason they received a Korean delegation at the Belper mills in September 1968. Dr Park Dong-Myo and Brigadier-General Kim Jung-Moo of the Korean Economic and Scientific Council, here with mill officials, spent two hours at the mill site.

First casualty of the mill clearances carried out by the English Sewing Cotton Company from 1959 was the unique Round Mill, the only industrial building ever to be built based on the panopticon principle where standing in the centre allows an overseer to see an entire floor. Built in 1811, it was already out of use by the start of the twentieth century, and its demolition began in November 1959. At lunchtime on 2 December, it suddenly collapsed, killing four workmen.

By 24 March 1962 work on the removal of the South Mill, floor by floor, was well advanced. The iron framework – revolutionary in its day – was open to the daylight as work progressed on the demolition. No hard hats in evidence, and everything removed by wheelbarrow, as the third floor gradually disappears.

In November 1962, after the South and West mills had been demolished, some of the redundant water channels were filled in, including that to the North Mill. Two years later a new mill canteen would be built, partly over the old mill race.

In May 1990, another of Belper's most distinctive landmarks was demolished, brick by brick. The mill chimney of 1854 had been declared unsafe after it swayed badly in high winds earlier in the year. Initially, bricks were dropped down the chimney, until it had been lowered sufficiently to use a chute.

After the particularly destructive year of 1962 in Belper, eyes turned to the unused mills at Milford. In February and March 1964 work began in earnest – here the east wing and clock tower of the Milford mills are seen in a state of demolition. Representatives of the English Sewing Cotton Company came out to inspect the clearance work on 7 March.

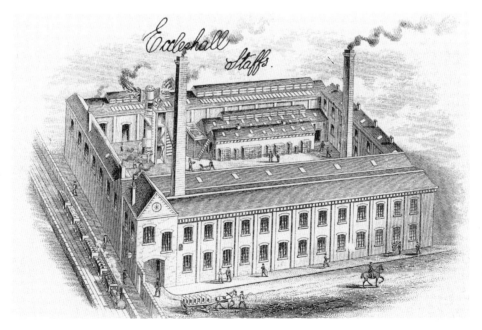

Starting on Queen Street, Park Foundry moved to this site on Bowling Alley, close to the railway cutting, in the mid-nineteenth century. The foundry finally outgrew these premises on what is now the Co-op car park, and moved in 1899 to Becksitch Lane, where the first new cast was made on Christmas Eve.

The foundries of Smedley Brothers operated in Belper from 1855 to September 1970. Here is part of the workforce from the Eagle Foundry on Becksitch Lane, before the end of the nineteenth century.

Foundry owners Smedley Brothers celebrated their 100th anniversary in the town with a dinner in the River Gardens pavilion on 2 December 1955. The younger generation of Smedleys are on the right – from the front, they are: Lillian; Donald; Audrey and Peter.

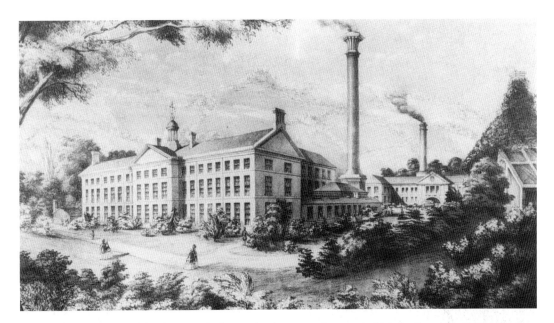

By 1844, the Ward family were the largest hosiery manufacturer in Britain. Based on either side of the Derby road, they employed 4,000 framework-knitters, who worked from home. After a fire destroyed their original warehouse, this replacement was built in 1850, close to Brook Cottage. As the nineteenth century progressed, production was moved on to the site, but Wards eventually went into liquidation in 1930. The Dalton family bought the site in 1934 and converted the warehouse and other buildings into an oil refinery. During 2004, the site was cleared, except for the warehouse and cottage, to allow for a new residential development.

Hosiery manufacturer Wards were officially Ward, Sturt and Sharp by the twentieth century. Here in the making-up room on 8 May 1911 are Fred Ault and Walter Burroughs supervising a large contingent of female workers.

Cutting out at Ward, Sturt and Sharp in 1911. Fred Ault (on the right) watches on. The company struggled to compete as the century progressed, closing in 1930.

The knitting section at Ward, Sturt and Sharp in 1923. On the left is Arthur Hallsworth – beside him is Arthur Hanson Jnr, son of the head mechanic.

After a four-day journey by road from Manchester, a giant boiler arrived for the Brettles dyeworks at Belper in November 1930. Weighing thirty tons, it was 30 ft long and moved on two bogey trailers pulled by a large steam engine. The boiler arrived in the late evening at Belper – local police would not allow it in the town until the following morning when hundreds watched its arrival.

A job well done for wheelwrights and blacksmiths at Wigley's forge on Field Lane, which stood opposite the present entrance to Field Lane car park.

Belper's Smithfield Cattle Market once stood on the site of the present Field Lane car park, to the rear of the Lion Garage site. Opening at the end of 1904, the market ran weekly all year round (except in times of foot and mouth outbreaks) until its eventual closure in October 1965.

The livestock weighing machine at the Belper Smithfield Cattle Market shortly after making its last weigh-in on 15 October 1965.

Demolition work was carried out on the Palace Cinema in King Street during July 1962. The building had stood exactly fifty years, having been built on the site of the Rose and Crown public house stables in 1912. It was replaced with Belper's first supermarket, Fine Fare, which opened in October 1963.

Packing Thornton's Easter eggs in the Derwent Street factory during March 1971 – the year of the firm's diamond jubilee. The factory had been established in Belper since 1947, although the opening of a second factory near Swanwick in the 1980s has gradually seen the Belper site used less, with closure expected in 2004/05.

Other local titles published by Tempus

Derbyshire in the 1930s A Lantern Slide Journey
DONALD ROOKSBY

This book of photographs takes the reader through some of the most scenic parts of Derbyshire as they looked in the mid-1930s. Pastoral scenes of farmland and dale follow views of towns and villages, and the county town itself, all looking quieter and calmer in those pre-war days than they do today.
07524 3258 3

Nottingham Pubs
DOUGLAS WHITWORTH

This book is a record of 200 of Nottingham's public houses past and present, sure to appeal to those interested in the history of Nottingham. In addition to the most historic hostelries, this selection of archive images also records many of the back street pubs which disappeared in the 1970s when whole districts of the city were cleared.
07524 3243 5

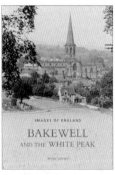

Bakewell and the White Peak
PETER TUFFREY

This collection of over 200 postcard views covers Bakewell and many of the surrounding villages, including Baslow, Calver, Grindleford and Rowsley. The images, taken by Edgar Leonard Scrivens, a leading exponent of the picture postcard during the first half of the twentieth century, show local views prior to industrial or commercial developments, from children playing in traffic-free streets to well-known landmarks like Mam Tor at Castleton.
07524 3042 4

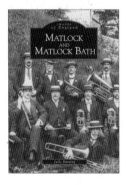

Matlock and Matlock Bath
JULIE BUNTING

This collection of archive images shows some of the diverse changes that have taken place in this area of the Peak District during the last century. The reader is given a glimpse of developments which have taken place in transport and industry; the shops and streets, and experiences of external events such as two world wars which have helped shape the nature of Matlock and Matlock Bath.
07524 2455 6

If you are interested in purchasing other books published by Tempus, or in case you have difficulty finding any Tempus books in your local bookshop, you can also place orders directly through our website
www.tempus-publishing.com